LIVING OUT LOUD

— ON —

PURPOSE!

STUDY WORKBOOK

Finding Your Voice, Embracing Your Identity, and Walking in Purpose

KAREN F. HATCHER

Printed in the United States of America
ISBN paperback: 978-1-968644-06-2
ISBN eBOOK: 978-1-968644-07-9

Library of Congress Control Number: 2026902195

River of Life Publishing
Memphis, Tennessee

A 14-session guided workbook designed to accompany the book *Living Out Loud on Purpose*, helping readers engage each chapter through study, discussion, reflection, and purpose-driven application.

TABLE OF CONTENTS

INTRODUCTION

You are beginning a journey that is more than a study; it is a transformation. This workbook is designed to walk beside you as you discover your voice, embrace your identity, and step boldly into your God-given purpose.

The book *Living Out Loud on Purpose* invites you to believe that nothing about you is accidental. Every experience, lesson, moment of bravery, and even every moment of fear has prepared you for such a time as this. This workbook helps you process those truths deeply, not just by reading, but by engaging, reflecting, writing, praying, and applying.

This is your space, your story, your becoming.

Each chapter of the workbook mirrors the themes in the main book, but here, you will move at a slower pace, stopping to ask hard questions, celebrate growth, confront patterns, and practice living with intention.

The tone and flow of this workbook come from two places:

1. The author's heart – warm, reflective, Spirit-led, and honest.

2. The structure of study – clear, practical, interactive, and purposeful.

You will see both throughout this workbook.

As you begin, remember:

- You are not here to be perfect; you are here to be present.

- You are not here to impress; you are here to grow.
- You are not here to rush; you are here to transform.

Come ready to be stretched. Come ready to be seen by God. Come ready to live out loud—on purpose.

HOW TO USE THIS WORKBOOK

This workbook is intentionally designed to help you apply the message of *Living Out Loud on Purpose* to your daily life. Whether you are completing this journey individually or with a group, here is how to get the most out of it:

1. Read the chapter in the main book first.
   The workbook is a companion, not a replacement. The book gives revelation; the workbook gives activation.

2. Begin each chapter with openness.
   Each chapter includes a "Reflection Warm-Up" to prepare your heart and focus your thoughts before engaging the deeper content.

3. Engage the interactive elements.
   Every chapter includes several components designed to help you process spiritually, emotionally, and practically:

   - Reflection Warm-Up
     A short mindset check to prepare your heart.
   - Chapter Summary
     A concise explanation of the chapter's theme.
   - Key Takeaways
     Essential truths to remember.

- Scripture Foundation
  Verses to anchor your study.
- Living Out Loud Reflection Questions
  Open-ended prompts to explore your story, habits, identity, and purpose.
- Purpose Practice
  A practical action step to help you apply the chapter's message this week.
- Voice & Identity Activation
  Prompts designed to build spiritual confidence and inner clarity.
- Journaling Space
  A safe place to process thoughts, scriptures, emotions, and prayers.

4. Write honestly and deeply.
   Your growth is tied to your willingness to be transparent with God and with yourself. Don't rush your answers. Sit with them. Let the Holy Spirit speak.

5. Use this workbook for both personal and group engagement. You may use this as:

   - Individual spiritual development
   - A women's ministry study
   - A discipleship program
   - A mentorship tool
   - A leadership development resource

6. Refer to the Facilitator Appendix (at the back) if you are leading others.

   A complete teaching appendix is included at the end of the workbook, containing:

   - Chapter teaching outlines
   - Discussion questions
   - Group activities
   - Prayer focuses
   - Leadership notes
   - Session timing suggestions

   These are NOT part of your participant pages and should not interrupt your personal journey.

7. End each chapter with prayer.
   Transformation happens when revelation meets surrender. Don't just read, pray through each chapter's theme.

8. Move at your own pace.
   This is not a race. Some seasons require slower work and deeper reflection. Give yourself grace to linger where you need healing or clarity.

9. Celebrate your progress.
   At the end of each chapter, a brief "Living Out Loud Check-In" encourages you to track your growth. Small steps count.

10. Prepare your heart for Bonus Chapter 14 — *Walk It Out*.
    This bonus chapter moves you from reflection into action. It challenges you to live what you've learned, practice intentional obedience, and consistently apply purpose in real life, not just in moments of inspiration, but in everyday choices.

You are ready. Now take a deep breath. Invite the Holy Spirit into this moment. Let every page meet you where you are and lead you to where God is calling you. You are not just studying purpose. You are stepping into it. Let's begin.

CHAPTER 1

YOU DID THAT ON PURPOSE

REFLECTION WARM-UP

Before you begin, take a moment to center your heart.

Ask yourself:

- What am I hoping God will reveal about my story today?
- Am I ready to look at my past through a new lens?
- Where do I feel unsure, unseen, or uncertain about purpose?

Take a deep breath. Invite the Holy Spirit to speak as you open this chapter.

CHAPTER SUMMARY

Life has a way of making us believe that our experiences are random, scattered, or meaningless. But Chapter 1 reminds us that God wastes nothing. Every moment—the beautiful, the painful, the confusing—has become part of your purpose.

You are not an accident. Your story isn't accidental. God has been intentional about you from the very beginning. What once looked like a mistake becomes meaningful when viewed through the eyes of purpose. This chapter invites you to revisit your story, not with shame or confusion, but with clarity, healing, and gratitude.

KEY TAKEAWAYS

- God is intentional. Nothing in your story is wasted.
- Your past has prepared you for your purpose.
- What you misunderstood may have been God's strategic shaping.
- You are living a story He designed with care, precision, and love.

SCRIPTURE FOUNDATION

- "All things work together for good" (Romans 8:28).
- "Before I formed you… I knew you" (Jeremiah 1:5).
- "All the days ordained for me were written" (Psalm 139:16).

REFLECTION QUESTIONS

Write freely. There are no wrong answers, only honest ones.

Which moments from your past now look different when you consider God's intentionality?

____

____

____

____

What experiences once felt painful or pointless, but now seem connected to your purpose?

____

____

____

____

Are there parts of your story you still struggle to accept? Why?

____

____

____

____

How might God be using your story to help others?

____

____

____

____

What lies about your past do you need to break the agreement with today?

____

____

____

____

PURPOSE PRACTICE

Take 10–12 minutes to write a Purpose Timeline.

Fill the table below with as many moments as come to mind. Don't overthink. Allow the Holy Spirit to highlight what matters. If you need more space, feel free to continue on a separate sheet of paper or in a journal.

1. Key Life Moments
2. What I Felt at That Time
3. What God May Have Been Doing

Key Life Moments	What I Felt at That Time	What God May Have Been Doing

IDENTITY & VOICE ACTIVATION

Complete the statements below:

"God was shaping me when______________________________."
"I now see purpose in______________________________."
"I survived ________________, and now I understand why."
"This part of my story doesn't define me; it____________."

Speak these aloud if you can. Your voice matters in reshaping your narrative.

APPLICATION EXERCISE — HEALING THE NARRATIVE

Write a letter to your younger self. One paragraph is enough, but you may write more.

Include:

- Validation
- Compassion
- What God was doing
- What God is still doing
- One affirmation rooted in Scripture

This is not therapy; it is clarity.

____

____

____

____

LIVING OUT LOUD CHECK-IN

Rate your heart in these areas today (1 = low, 5 = strong):

AREA	1	2	3	4	5
I believe God is intentional about my life.	☐	☐	☐	☐	☐
I see purpose in parts of my story.	☐	☐	☐	☐	☐
I trust God with the parts I don't understand.	☐	☐	☐	☐	☐
I am ready to embrace my story without fear.	☐	☐	☐	☐	☐

GROWTH THOUGHT FOR THE WEEK

When God does something "on purpose," it is neither haphazard nor careless. What He does, and what He allows, is deliberate, meaningful, and rooted in His infinite wisdom and love.

CLOSING PRAYER

Father, thank You for being intentional with my life. Help me see my story through Your eyes. Heal what still hurts, clarify what still confuses me, and reveal the purpose behind every step I've taken. Make me confident in the truth that You have always been with me, guiding, shaping, preparing, and loving me on purpose. Amen.

LIVING OUT LOUD PAGES

Write honestly. Speak freely. Respond intentionally.

Use this space to process anything God is revealing.

CHAPTER 2

PURPOSE: THE AGE-OLD QUESTION

REFLECTION WARM-UP

Before you begin, pause for a moment.

Close your eyes and ask yourself:

- What have I believed about purpose, and where did those beliefs come from?
- Has purpose felt confusing, intimidating, or out of reach?
- What do I hope God clarifies in this chapter?

Breathe deeply. Release any pressure to "figure out everything." Purpose is revealed one faithful step at a time.

CHAPTER SUMMARY

Purpose is not a puzzle you must solve; it is a journey God invites you to walk. It unfolds in seasons, layers, and stages.

In this chapter, you learn that purpose is not something you chase; it is something God reveals as you grow, obey, and align with Him. You were created with intent, designed with intention, and shaped on purpose. Purpose is not found in striving; it is found in God. As you walk with Him, clarity increases and confusion breaks.

This chapter calls you to release the fear, pressure, and comparison around purpose so you can see clearly what God is doing in your life right now.

KEY TAKEAWAYS

- Purpose is discovered through relationship, not performance.
- You were created with intention; there is no randomness in God's design.
- Purpose unfolds gradually as you follow God's lead.
- You are already walking in parts of your purpose without realizing it.

SCRIPTURE FOUNDATION

- God's plans are good, intentional, and full of hope (Jeremiah 29:11).
- God's purpose prevails over human plans (Proverbs 19:21).
- The steps of a good person are ordered by the Lord (Psalm 37:23).

REFLECTION QUESTIONS

Take your time with these. Purpose becomes clearer when you slow down enough to listen.

What misconceptions about purpose have shaped your thinking?

____

____

____

____

Has fear ever made you feel unqualified for purpose? Why?

____

____

____

____

What small signs of purpose has God already revealed in your life?

____

____

____

____

How has comparison affected your confidence or clarity?

____

____

____

____

What activities, gifts, or roles make you feel most aligned with who God created you to be?

____

____

____

____

PURPOSE PRACTICE

Create Your Purpose Snapshot

This exercise prepares your heart to receive clarity throughout the rest of the workbook.

In three short sections, write your current understanding of purpose:

What I Believe God Created Me to Do (Right Now)

(Write what feels true today, even if it's simple or incomplete.)

____

____

____

____

What I Sense God Stirring in Me for the Future
(Dreams, nudges, ideas, burdens, passions)

____

____

____

____

What I Need God to Clarify
(Areas where you feel uncertain or overwhelmed)

____

____

____

____

IDENTITY & VOICE ACTIVATION

Speak (or write) these statements of alignment:

- "My purpose is unfolding, and I don't have to rush it."
- "God created me with intention. I am not random."
- "My gifts point toward my calling."
- "God's purpose for me will prevail."

Now write your own declaration beginning with: "I was created to…"

____

____

____

____

Let your spirit respond before your mind edits.

APPLICATION EXERCISE: MAPPING THE SEEDS OF PURPOSE

Grab a blank space or page. Draw a simple tree. Then label:

1. **ROOTS**

   What foundations in your life have shaped you? (Values, lessons, trials, upbringing, mentors, spiritual truths)

____

____

____

____

2. **TRUNK**

What strengths or skills support your purpose?
(Leadership, compassion, creativity, intercession,
teaching, encouragement)

____

____

____

____

3. **BRANCHES**

Where is your purpose extending or expressing itself
right now?
(Family, ministry, career, community, relationships)

____

____

____

____

4. FRUIT

What impact do you hope God produces through your life?

____

____

____

____

This visual exercise helps you *see* that you are already walking in purpose.

LIVING OUT LOUD CHECK-IN

How confident do you feel today in understanding your purpose?

Circle or check the number that reflects you now:

AREA	1	2	3	4	5
I believe God has a clear purpose for my life.	☐	☐	☐	☐	☐
I feel connected to at least part of my purpose.	☐	☐	☐	☐	☐
I believe purpose is unfolding in seasons.	☐	☐	☐	☐	☐

AREA   **1 2 3 4 5**

I trust God to reveal the next step in His timing.   ☐ ☐ ☐ ☐ ☐

GROWTH THOUGHT FOR THE WEEK

Living out loud is evidence that purpose has been discovered.

CLOSING PRAYER

Lord, thank You for creating me with intention. Quiet every voice that brings fear, pressure, or confusion. Reveal purpose to me step by step, season by season. Help me walk boldly in what I know and trust You with what I don't. Align my heart with Your plans and let my life bring You glory. In Jesus' name. Amen.

LIVING OUT LOUD PAGES

Write honestly. Speak freely. Respond intentionally.

Journal anything God is highlighting about your purpose.

CHAPTER 3

BECOMING: EMBRACING THE PROCESS OF PURPOSE

REFLECTION WARM-UP

Before diving into this chapter, pause and reflect.

Consider these questions:

- Where in my life do I feel God stretching me?
- What parts of the process frustrate or intimidate me?
- Am I willing to grow, even when growth feels uncomfortable?

Growth is holy. Becoming is sacred. You are right where God intends for you to be.

CHAPTER SUMMARY

Becoming is not a moment; it is a lifelong process. Every season you have walked through has shaped, refined, and stretched you into who God is calling you to be. Sometimes becoming feels uncomfortable, slow, or hidden. But hidden seasons are often where God does His most powerful work.

In this chapter, you are invited to embrace the truth that you are a work in progress. God is forming, pruning, healing, strengthening, and preparing you. Nothing in the process is wasted.

The journey of becoming is both beautiful and challenging, but it is always purposeful.

KEY TAKEAWAYS

- Becoming is continuous; God shapes you through every season.
- You are not behind; you are being refined.
- Growth requires stretching, surrender, and patience.
- God uses process to prepare you for purpose.

SCRIPTURE FOUNDATION

- God will finish the work He started in you (Philippians 1:6).
- God is the potter; we are the clay (Isaiah 64:8).
- God prunes what is fruitful so it can bear more fruit (John 15:2).

REFLECTION QUESTIONS

Slow down with these. Becoming requires honesty.

What season of becoming are you currently in (healing, stretching, preparing, pruning, rebuilding, restoring)?

____

____

What has been the hardest part of the process for you, and why?

Where have you seen growth in yourself that you once thought was impossible?

What old habits, fears, or mindsets is God pruning from your life?

____

____

____

____

What new disciplines or perspectives is God forming within you?

____

____

____

____

PURPOSE PRACTICE

Write Your "Becoming" Statement

Use one sentence to summarize what God is shaping in you right now. Start with:

"In this season, God is forming in me…"

Examples:

- "In this season, God is forming in me a stronger prayer life."

- "In this season, God is forming in me the courage to walk in purpose."
- "In this season, God is forming in me emotional maturity."
- "In this season, God is forming in me humility and trust."

Let it be honest. Let it be real.

____

____

IDENTITY & VOICE ACTIVATION

Complete the following:

"I am becoming someone who_____________________."
"God is strengthening me in_____________________."
"I release the pressure to be perfect in_____________________."
"I embrace the process because_____________________."

These statements retrain the heart to accept growth without shame.

APPLICATION EXERCISE: THE REFINING CHART

Draw a simple two-column chart.

Column A: "What God Is Removing"
Write down anything God is pruning in your life.
(Fear, impatience, insecurity, perfectionism, old habits, negative voices.)

Column B: "What God Is Making Room For"
Write what you sense God is replacing those things with.
(Peace, courage, discipline, identity, clarity, faith, boldness.)
This practice helps you see the beauty in God's refining work.

LIVING OUT LOUD CHECK-IN

How are you experiencing the process of becoming this week?

Rate each statement:

AREA	1	2	3	4	5
I trust God's process, even when it feels slow.	☐	☐	☐	☐	☐
I see areas of growth in myself.	☐	☐	☐	☐	☐
I am willing to let God prune what no longer serves my purpose.	☐	☐	☐	☐	☐
I believe God is forming something new in me.	☐	☐	☐	☐	☐

GROWTH THOUGHT FOR THE WEEK

The process is part of the purpose.

CLOSING PRAYER

Father, thank You for being patient with me in every season. Teach me to trust Your process, even when I do not understand it. Prune what needs to be released and strengthen what You are building in me. Help me embrace becoming with grace, courage, and surrender. Form me into who You designed me to be… one step at a time. Amen.

LIVING OUT LOUD PAGES

Write honestly. Speak freely. Respond intentionally.

Write freely about where God is shaping, stretching, and refining you.

CHAPTER 4

ON DISPLAY: WHEN PURPOSE GOES PUBLIC

REFLECTION WARM-UP

Visibility can bring excitement… or anxiety.

Before beginning, ask yourself:

- How do I feel about being seen?
- Do I shy away from visibility because of fear or past hurt?
- What might God be calling me to step into publicly?

Give yourself permission to be honest. This chapter touches identity, confidence, and assignment.

CHAPTER SUMMARY

When God brings you "on display," it is never about spotlight; it is about stewardship. Your life becomes a visible testimony of His goodness, wisdom, and work in you.

Being seen is not about being celebrated.
Being seen is not about being perfect.

Being seen is not about performance.

When God elevates, promotes, or positions you publicly, He is showcasing His glory through your life. This chapter helps you release fear, embrace divine assignment, and trust that God equips you for every platform He places beneath your feet.

KEY TAKEAWAYS

- Visibility is assignment, not attention.
- God uses your story publicly to help others privately.
- When God positions you, He strengthens you.
- Your confidence should come from God, not people's opinions.

SCRIPTURE FOUNDATION

- Let your light shine before others (Matthew 5:14-16).
- You are chosen to declare God's praises (1 Peter 2:9).
- Be strong and courageous; God is with you (Joshua 1:9).

REFLECTION QUESTIONS

Write freely, honestly, and without judgment.

What feelings arise when you think about being "on display"?

____

____

____

____

Has fear of criticism or insecurity held you back from stepping into visibility?

What platforms or opportunities do you sense God preparing you for?

What has God already placed in you that others need to see?

____

____

What would change if you viewed visibility as ministry rather than pressure?

____

____

____

____

PURPOSE PRACTICE

Your Assignment Inventory

Write down areas where God may be increasing your visibility:

- Ministry
- Leadership
- Community work
- Career
- Creativity
- Family influence
- Prayer or intercession
- Mentoring
- Business or entrepreneurship

Then answer these questions:

What scares me about stepping forward?

____

____

____

____

What excites me about stepping forward?

____

____

____

____

What is one small step I can take this week toward showing up more boldly?

____

____

____

Visibility grows through intentional steps.

IDENTITY & VOICE ACTIVATION

Make these declarations:

- "God is positioning me, and I won't shrink back."
- "I am not on display for attention; I am on display for purpose."
- "I will not hide what God has placed within me."
- "I embrace divine opportunities with confidence and humility."

Now create your own statement beginning with:
"When God calls me forward, I will…"

Let confidence rise as you write.

____

____

APPLICATION EXERCISE: FACING THE FEAR OF VISIBILITY

Sometimes visibility feels threatening because of past hurt or present insecurity.

In the two boxes below, write:
Box 1: "What Visibility Makes Me Fear"
Write every fear, worry, or negative thought that surfaces.

Examples:
- "I might fail."

- "People will judge me."
- "I don't feel qualified."
- "I don't want attention."

Box 2: "What God Says About My Visibility"
Combat each fear with Scripture or truth.

Examples:
- "I am equipped."
- "God is with me."
- "I am chosen for this moment."
- "My story will help someone else."

Let this exercise shift your perspective.

Box 1: What Visibility Makes Me Fear

Box 2: What God Says About My Visibility

LIVING OUT LOUD CHECK-IN

How ready do you feel to embrace visibility this week?

Rate yourself:

AREA	1	2	3	4	5
I see visibility as an assignment, not pressure.	☐	☐	☐	☐	☐
I feel capable of stepping into new platforms.	☐	☐	☐	☐	☐
I believe God equips me when He elevates me.	☐	☐	☐	☐	☐
I am ready to stop shrinking and start showing up.	☐	☐	☐	☐	☐

GROWTH THOUGHT FOR THE WEEK

Visibility is not about vanity. It is about stewardship.

CLOSING PRAYER

Lord, when You call me forward, help me walk boldly. Release me from fear, insecurity, and self-doubt. Let my life reflect Your goodness everywhere I go. Position me where You want me, use me how You desire, and let Your glory shine through every platform You give me. Amen.

LIVING OUT LOUD PAGES

Write honestly. Speak freely. Respond intentionally.

Reflect on a time God pushed you forward when you wanted to stay hidden.

____

____

____

____

____

____

____

____

____

____

CHAPTER 5

RESPONDING VS. REACTING: LIVING WITH DISCERNMENT AND DISCIPLINE

REFLECTION WARM-UP

Take a moment to breathe deeply. This chapter invites honesty and self-awareness.

Ask yourself:

- Do I tend to react quickly when I feel hurt or pressured?
- Where do my emotional triggers come from?
- How would my relationships and purpose grow if I responded with wisdom instead of reaction?

Give yourself permission to grow in emotional strength.

CHAPTER SUMMARY

Responding and reacting may look similar on the outside, but they come from very different places internally.

Reaction is immediate. It is emotional, impulsive, and often rooted in past wounds, fear, or insecurity.

Response is intentional. It is guided by the Holy Spirit, shaped by wisdom, and rooted in emotional maturity.

In this chapter, you learn that fulfilling your purpose requires discipline, especially in how you handle frustration, conflict, disappointment, and unexpected moments. You cannot live out loud on purpose if your emotions constantly lead your decisions. God is calling you to steadiness, not instability, to discernment, not impulsiveness, to peace, not panic.

KEY TAKEAWAYS

- Reactions come from emotion. Responses come from wisdom.
- Emotional maturity is essential for purpose.
- You have the Holy Spirit to guide your decisions.
- You can pause, breathe, and choose wisely; you are not controlled by your emotions.

SCRIPTURE FOUNDATION

- Be quick to listen, slow to speak, slow to become angry (James 1:19).
- A gentle answer turns away wrath (Proverbs 15:1).
- Self-control is a fruit of the Spirit (Galatians 5:22-23).

REFLECTION QUESTIONS

Reflect with patience and honesty; growth requires truth.

What kinds of situations tend to trigger emotional reactions for you?

What past hurts, memories, or patterns might influence your reactions?

How do you feel physically and spiritually when you react instead of respond?

What is one situation recently where you wish you had responded differently?

____

____

____

____

What would responding with wisdom look like in your relationships, leadership, or calling?

____

____

____

____

PURPOSE PRACTICE

The PAUSE Exercise

Answer each question of the word P.A.U.S.E on each line for yourself:

P – Pause. What can you stop and breathe through before reacting?

____

____

____

____

A – Acknowledge. What emotion are you actually feeling?

____

____

____

____

U – Understand. Why does this trigger affect you?

____

____

____

S – Seek Wisdom. What does Scripture or the Holy Spirit say to do?

____

____

____

____

E – Execute. What wise response can you choose instead?

____

____

____

____

This tool helps retrain your emotional responses.

IDENTITY & VOICE ACTIVATION

Speak these statements aloud if possible:

- "I have control over my responses; my emotions do not rule me."
- "My reactions will not sabotage my purpose."
- "The Holy Spirit guides my decisions."
- "I choose wisdom over impulse."

Now write your own declaration beginning with:
"I will respond with intention when…"

Finish the sentence about a real situation you face.

APPLICATION EXERCISE: TRIGGERS & TRUTHS

In the two columns below:

Column A: "My Triggers"
List people, situations, words, or behaviors that cause strong emotional reactions.

Column B: "My Truths"
For each trigger, write a truth that brings calm, grounding, and perspective.

Example:

Trigger	Truth
Being misunderstood	God understands me fully.
Feeling ignored	My worth is not dependent on attention.
Being corrected	Correction helps me grow.

Trigger	Truth

This exercise builds emotional resilience.

LIVING OUT LOUD CHECK-IN

Rate your emotional posture this week:

AREA	1	2	3	4	5
I slow down before reacting.	☐	☐	☐	☐	☐
I am learning emotional discipline.	☐	☐	☐	☐	☐
I listen for the Holy Spirit before responding.	☐	☐	☐	☐	☐
I believe responding wisely honors my purpose.	☐	☐	☐	☐	☐

GROWTH THOUGHT FOR THE WEEK

Reactions are rooted in the flesh; responses are rooted in the Spirit.

CLOSING PRAYER

Holy Spirit, govern my emotions. Teach me to pause before I react. Give me wisdom before words, patience before decisions, and peace in every situation I face. Heal my triggers and strengthen my response. Lead me in maturity so I can fulfill the purpose You've placed within me. Amen.

LIVING OUT LOUD PAGES

Write honestly. Speak freely. Respond intentionally.

Write about a recent moment where you responded well, or where you wish you had.

What is God teaching you through it?

____

____

____

____

____

____

____

____

____

CHAPTER 6

IDENTITY: REMEMBER WHO YOU ARE

REFLECTION WARM-UP

Identity is deep work. Before you begin, take a moment to breathe and quiet your mind.

Ask yourself:

- What identities have I embraced that were never mine?
- Whose voice have I allowed to shape how I see myself: God's or people's?
- Am I ready for God to redefine how I see *me*?

Let your heart settle. Invite God to speak truth, not labels.

CHAPTER SUMMARY

Identity is the foundation of purpose. Before God reveals *what* you are called to do, He establishes *who* you are. Many of the spiritual battles you face are rooted in identity because the Enemy knows that if you ever fully believe who God says you are, you become unstoppable.

This chapter walks you through confronting false labels, breaking agreement with old narratives, releasing false identities, and embracing your God-given identity with confidence and clarity.

God is not trying to change you into someone else. He is calling you to become who He *originally* designed.

KEY TAKEAWAYS

- Identity comes from God, not people, performance, or past experiences.
- The Enemy attacks identity because it shapes confidence and purpose.
- Knowing who you are in Christ brings stability, authority, and clarity.
- You must release lies to embrace truth.

SCRIPTURE FOUNDATION

- You are chosen, royal, and set apart (1 Peter 2:9).
- Christ lives in you (Galatians 2:20).
- You are God's workmanship (Ephesians 2:10).
- You are a child of God (John 1:12).

REFLECTION QUESTIONS

Identity work is sacred—write with honesty and courage.

What labels or names have you carried that did not come from God?

____

____

____

____

Who or what shaped your understanding of yourself growing up?

____

____

____

____

What moments or experiences damaged your sense of identity?

____

____

____

____

What part of your God-given identity do you struggle to fully accept?

____

____

____

____

Where has the Enemy tried hardest to confuse or attack your identity?

____

____

____

____

PURPOSE PRACTICE

The "I AM" Identity Exercise

Write at least five identity statements based on Scripture, not emotion.

Example prompts:
- "I am chosen because…"
- "I am loved even when…"

- "I am called to…"
- "I am strengthened through…"
- "I am forgiven and free from…"

____

____

____

____

____

Then choose one statement, circle it, and commit to speaking it aloud daily this week. Your identity grows stronger the more you align your voice with God's truth.

IDENTITY & VOICE ACTIVATION

Complete these statements to declare identity over your life:

- "I release the old label of______________________."
- "I break agreement with the lie that says_______."
- "God calls me_________________________."
- "I am stepping into the identity of__________."
- "I am no longer defined by_______________."

Speak these aloud if possible. Your voice carries spiritual authority.

APPLICATION EXERCISE: FALSE LABELS VS. TRUTH LABELS

Column A: "False Labels"

Write every identity you've carried that is not from God.

Examples:
- "Not enough"
- "Too emotional"
- "Unworthy"
- "Unqualified"
- "Broken"
- "Too much"
- "Invisible"

Column B: "Truth Labels"
Rewrite each one using Scripture-based identity.

Examples:
- "I am fearfully and wonderfully made."
- "I am equipped and empowered."
- "I am seen and valued."
- "I am whole and healed through Christ."

This exercise uproots lies and replaces them with truth.

False Labels	Truth Labels

LIVING OUT LOUD CHECK-IN

How firmly are you standing in your God-given identity?

Rate yourself:

AREA	1	2	3	4	5
I believe the identity God has spoken over me.	☐	☐	☐	☐	☐
I am releasing old labels and false identities.	☐	☐	☐	☐	☐
I feel more confident in who God created me to be.	☐	☐	☐	☐	☐
I am beginning to walk in my true identity daily.	☐	☐	☐	☐	☐

GROWTH THOUGHT FOR THE WEEK

You can't live out loud if you don't know who is talking

CLOSING PRAYER

Father, restore my identity. Silence every lie that ever shaped my self-perception. Remove every label that does not come from You. Help me see myself through Your eyes: chosen, loved, equipped, and called. Let my confidence rise from truth, not fear. Anchor me in who You say I am… and let nothing uproot it. Amen.

LIVING OUT LOUD PAGES

Write honestly. Speak freely. Respond intentionally.

Write about the identity God is restoring in you.

____

____

____

____

____

____

____

____

____

____

____

CHAPTER 7

VOICE: YOU WERE NEVER MEANT TO BE SILENT

REFLECTION WARM-UP

Before beginning, still your heart and think about this:

- When was the last time you truly used your voice with confidence?
- What moments in your life made you feel unheard, dismissed, or silenced?
- How does God want to use your voice in this season?

Your voice is not small.
Your voice is not accidental.
Your voice is necessary.

CHAPTER SUMMARY

God gave you a voice for a reason. Your voice carries power, authority, healing, revelation, and testimony. But the Enemy works hard to silence it because he knows the power of a believer who speaks boldly and truthfully.

Silence often grows from fear, shame, insecurity, trauma, comparison, or past rejection. But this chapter reminds you that your voice is part of your divine identity. It is a weapon and a gift. When you speak what God has placed in your spirit, you shift atmospheres, encourage others, destroy lies, and advance the kingdom.

This chapter invites you to reclaim your voice, strengthen your confidence, and speak boldly, not for your glory, but for God's purpose.

KEY TAKEAWAYS

- Your voice is part of your calling and identity.
- The Enemy tries to silence the voices that carry power.
- God puts His words in your mouth, not your insecurities.
- Your testimony has the power to free others.
- Speaking boldly is an act of obedience.

SCRIPTURE FOUNDATION

- God puts His words in your mouth (Jeremiah 1:9).
- We overcome through testimony (Revelation 12:11).
- Speak up for those who cannot speak for themselves (Proverbs 31:8-9).
- God has not given a spirit of fear (2 Timothy 1:7).

REFLECTION QUESTIONS

Be honest. Your voice will grow stronger as you answer deeply.

What experiences, fears, or people have tried to silence your voice?

____

____

____

____

How has silence affected your relationships, leadership, or confidence?

____

____

____

____

When have you regretted not speaking up?

____

____

____

____

Where do you sense God calling you to use your voice more boldly?

____

____

____

____

What message or testimony has God entrusted you with?

____

____

____

____

PURPOSE PRACTICE

Write Your Voice Assignment

Take a few moments to prayerfully answer: "What has God placed in my mouth for this season?"

This might be:
- A message
- A testimony
- A teaching
- A prayer assignment

- A ministry
- A story you're finally ready to tell
- A truth you must speak in your home, workplace, or community

Write it boldly — your voice has purpose.

____

____

____

____

IDENTITY & VOICE ACTIVATION

Speak these declarations aloud, with strength:

- "My voice carries weight and authority."
- "What God placed in me will not be silenced."
- "I speak with clarity, boldness, and purpose."
- "My voice is a weapon against darkness."
- "I do not shrink; I speak."

Now write your own statement:
"I am stepping into my voice by…"

Describe the next step God is calling you to take.

____

____

____

75

____

APPLICATION EXERCISE: BREAKING THE SILENCE

SECTION 1: "WHAT SILENCED ME"

List moments, environments, or beliefs that caused you to hide your voice. This exercise frees what fear tried to shut down.

Examples:
- Being mocked
- Being overlooked
- Childhood silence
- Past rejection
- Feeling unqualified
- Intimidation
- Emotional wounds

____

____

____

____

____

____

____

____

SECTION 2: "WHAT FREES MY VOICE"

Write truths, scriptures, and revelations that empower you to speak.

Examples:
- "God has put His words in my mouth."
- "My voice helps others."
- "My story carries healing."
- "Silence is no longer my identity."
- "I speak with authority and grace."

____

____

____

____

____

____

LIVING OUT LOUD CHECK-IN

Rate your confidence in using your voice:

AREA	1	2	3	4	5
I believe my voice matters.	☐	☐	☐	☐	☐
I am growing more confident in speaking up.	☐	☐	☐	☐	☐
I feel ready to use my voice in new ways.	☐	☐	☐	☐	☐
I believe God will speak through me.	☐	☐	☐	☐	☐

GROWTH THOUGHT FOR THE WEEK

Your voice is a weapon, a witness, and a vessel of purpose.

CLOSING PRAYER

Lord, thank You for giving me a voice. Break every chain, silence, and insecurity that once held it captive. Speak through me boldly and clearly. Let my voice bring healing, truth, and light into every space I enter. Help me walk confidently in the assignment You have placed in my mouth. Amen.

LIVING OUT LOUD PAGES
Write honestly. Speak freely. Respond intentionally.

Write about a moment when using your voice changed something, in you or in someone else.

CHAPTER 8

FIREPROOF: STANDING WHEN IT'S HARD

REFLECTION WARM-UP

Hard seasons can leave emotional ash behind. Before beginning, ask yourself gently:

- What "fire" am I currently walking through?
- How do I usually respond to pressure or adversity?
- Where have I seen God strengthen me through past trials?

Take a breath. You are not alone in the fire. God is with you.

CHAPTER SUMMARY

This chapter reminds you that the fire is never sent to destroy you; it is sent to refine, strengthen, and mature you. Everything you have walked through, including the pressure and heat of life, has produced something powerful in you. Like the three Hebrew boys, you are never alone in the fire. God steps into it with you. Trials reveal what is essential and burn away what is not. Pressure produces perseverance. Adversity shapes authority.

Struggle strengthens your spiritual stamina. You are not fragile; you are fireproof.

KEY TAKEAWAYS

- Trials produce spiritual maturity and endurance.
- God is present in every fire, even when He feels silent.
- Fire reveals strength, character, and purpose.
- You come out stronger when you walk through adversity with God.

SCRIPTURE FOUNDATION

- You will walk through the fire and not be burned (Isaiah 43:2)
- God is with you in the fire (Daniel 3:25).
- Trials refine your faith like gold (1 Peter 1:7).
- Suffering produces endurance, character, and hope (Romans 5:3-4).

REFLECTION QUESTIONS

Write your answers honestly. This chapter invites vulnerability and healing.

What difficult season has shaped you the most, and how?

____

____

____

____

When have you felt God's presence in the middle of a storm or trial?

____

____

____

____

What fears rise up in you when life gets hard?

____

____

____

____

How has adversity strengthened your purpose or character?

____

____

____

____

What "fire" are you currently facing, and what might God be refining?

____

____

____

____

PURPOSE PRACTICE

The Fireproof Faith Exercise
List your three biggest past challenges or trials.

For each one, answer these three questions:

1. What was the fire?
2. How did it feel at the time?
3. What strength or wisdom did it produce in me?

This helps you recognize the spiritual muscles God built in adversity.

____

____

____

____

____

____

____

____

____

____

____

IDENTITY & VOICE ACTIVATION

Speak or write these declarations:

- "This fire will not consume me; it will refine me."
- "God is with me in every trial."
- "What was meant to break me will build me."
- "I am fire-tested and God-protected."

Now complete this sentence:
"I will come out of this fire with…"

____

____

(Fill in with qualities like strength, clarity, maturity, courage, healing, testimony.)

APPLICATION EXERCISE: REFINING HEAT MAP

In the space below, draw a circle and label it "The Fire I'm Facing."

Then draw branches outward and label them:

- What this fire is teaching me
- What this fire is strengthening in me
- What this fire is burning away
- What this fire is preparing me for
- Where I see God in the midst of it

This visual reflection reveals that trials are purposeful, not punitive.

LIVING OUT LOUD CHECK-IN

How are you navigating difficult seasons right now?

Rate yourself:

AREA	1	2	3	4	5
I believe God is with me in every fire.	☐	☐	☐	☐	☐
I feel stronger because of past trials.	☐	☐	☐	☐	☐
I trust God to refine, not destroy me.	☐	☐	☐	☐	☐
I am learning to stand with faith under pressure.	☐	☐	☐	☐	☐

GROWTH THOUGHT FOR THE WEEK

The fire doesn't destroy your purpose; it forges it.

CLOSING PRAYER

Father, thank You for being present in every fire I face. Strengthen my faith when life feels overwhelming. Teach me to trust Your refining work. Burn away what no longer serves my purpose. Let endurance rise, courage grow, and wisdom deepen in me. I declare that I will come out of every fire stronger, wiser, and more aligned with Your will. Amen.

LIVING OUT LOUD PAGES

Write honestly. Speak freely. Respond intentionally.

Write about a time when God brought you through something you thought would break you, but instead made you stronger.

____

____

____

____

____

____

____

____

____

____

CHAPTER 9

LIVING OUT LOUD: THE COST OF THE CALL

REFLECTION WARM-UP

Before beginning, take a moment to reflect with honesty and courage.

Ask yourself:

- What has following God *already* cost me?
- Where do I feel stretched, challenged, or uncomfortable in this season?
- Am I willing to let go of what God is asking me to release?

Purpose is beautiful, but costly. God never calls without preparing and stretching the one He calls.

CHAPTER SUMMARY

The call of God is powerful, purposeful, and deeply fulfilling, but it also comes with a price. To walk in your calling, you must release what no longer fits, obey even when it's uncomfortable, and trust God when the cost feels high.

Sacrifice is not punishment.
Sacrifice is preparation.

In this chapter, you learn that the cost of the call is part of spiritual maturity. God will not ask you to give up anything without offering something greater in return: clarity, strength, discipline, alignment, and supernatural growth.

Purpose requires your "yes." But your "yes" requires faith.

KEY TAKEAWAYS

- God calls you to a higher standard, and higher standards cost something.
- You cannot carry old habits, relationships, or mindsets into a new season.
- Sacrifice is evidence that God is trusting you with more.
- Your obedience unlocks doors that fear tries to keep shut.

SCRIPTURE FOUNDATION

- Deny yourself, take up your cross, and follow Me (Luke 9:23).
- Present your body as a living sacrifice (Romans 12:1).
- Press toward the mark; let go of the past (Philippians 3:13-14).

- Obedience is better than sacrifice (1 Samuel 15:22).

REFLECTION QUESTIONS

These questions may challenge you; lean into them with honesty.

What has following God required you to release, leave, or change?

____

____

____

____

How has sacrifice strengthened your relationship with God?

____

____

____

What part of the call feels most costly right now?

____

____

____

____

What comforts or patterns has God asked you to outgrow?

____

____

____

____

Where do you sense God calling you to deeper obedience?

____

____

____

____

PURPOSE PRACTICE

Your Surrender Inventory

This practice helps align your heart with God's direction.

Create two sections.

SECTION 1: "WHAT I AM HOLDING"

Write down anything you're struggling to release: habits, people, comfort zones, fears, responsibilities, roles, identities, or behaviors.

SECTION 2: "WHAT GOD IS ASKING FOR"

Write down what the Holy Spirit is nudging you to surrender. Then finish with: "Lord, I trust You with the cost."

IDENTITY & VOICE ACTIVATION

Declare these statements; they reshape how you understand sacrifice:

- "Obedience is not loss; it is alignment."

- "God will never take something without giving purpose in return."
- "My calling is worth the cost."
- "I release what no longer serves my assignment."
- "My 'yes' makes room for God's best."

Now, complete this personal declaration: "One thing I am willing to surrender so I can grow is…"

____

Let it be real. Let it be honest.

APPLICATION EXERCISE: THE EXCHANGE TABLE

Draw a table with two columns:

Column A: "What It Costs"
List the things you feel God is asking you to release.

Examples:
- Comfort
- Control
- Old friendships
- Fear of rejection
- Busyness
- People-pleasing
- Procrastination
- Old habits

Column B: "What I Gain"
Write what God is offering in place of each sacrifice.

Examples:
- Clarity
- Peace
- Growth
- New relationships
- Influence
- Confidence
- Healing
- Purpose alignment

Seeing the exchange helps you embrace the beauty of obedience.

LIVING OUT LOUD CHECK-IN

How are you embracing the cost of your calling?

Rate yourself:

AREA	1	2	3	4	5
I understand that purpose requires sacrifice.	☐	☐	☐	☐	☐
I am willing to release what no longer aligns with my calling.	☐	☐	☐	☐	☐
I trust God with the cost of obedience.	☐	☐	☐	☐	☐
I see surrender as a path to growth, not loss.	☐	☐	☐	☐	☐

GROWTH THOUGHT FOR THE WEEK

Purpose demands more from you because God intends to do more through you

CLOSING PRAYER

Father, give me the courage to surrender whatever You ask of me. Strengthen my "yes" when it feels costly. Help me release what no longer fits my assignment. Let obedience reshape my life, purpose, and faith. May every sacrifice become a seed for growth, clarity, and alignment. My calling is worth the cost, and I trust You completely. Amen.

LIVING OUT LOUD PAGES

Write honestly. Speak freely. Respond intentionally.

Write about a time when obeying God cost you something, but in the end, it grew you.

CHAPTER 10

LIVING OUT LOUD: REDEFINED

REFLECTION WARM-UP

Take a moment to settle your spirit.

Ask yourself:

- What does "living out loud" mean to me personally?
- Where in my life am I still shrinking, hiding, or dimming my light?
- Am I willing to live authentically, even if it stretches me?

Let go of the idea that boldness means being loud. Boldness begins in the heart.

CHAPTER SUMMARY

Living out loud is not about volume, attention, or performance. It is about authenticity, alignment, courage, and obedience.

This chapter redefines "living out loud" as living boldly in the identity, purpose, gifts, and calling God placed within you, without apology, comparison, or fear. The boldness God calls you to is not based on personality, but on intimacy with Him.

You were created to live fully, freely, and visibly in the will of God, not hidden, muted, or diminished. Living out loud means stepping into who God created you to be—unashamed, unrestricted, and unshrinking.

KEY TAKEAWAYS

- Living out loud is about authenticity, not attention.
- Boldness flows from identity and intimacy with God.
- Fear cannot coexist with purpose; one must bow.
- God has called you to show up fully, not halfway.
- Your life becomes a witness when you stop shrinking.

SCRIPTURE FOUNDATION

- God gave you power, love, and a sound mind (2 Timothy 1:7).
- Let your light shine (Matthew 5:16).
- The righteous are bold as a lion (Proverbs 28:1).
- The Lord is your light and salvation; whom shall you fear? (Psalm 27:1).

REFLECTION QUESTIONS

Answer with honesty; this chapter may expose places where fear once lived.

What areas of your life do you tend to shrink back in, and why?

____

____

____

____

How would your life look different if you fully embraced who God created you to be?

____

____

____

____

What does "authentic boldness" look like for you personally?

____

____

____

____

What fears keep you from living boldly and out loud?

____

____

____

____

What parts of your purpose are waiting for your confidence to catch up?

____

____

____

____

PURPOSE PRACTICE
"No More Shrinking" Exercise

In two sections, write:

SECTION 1: "WHERE I'VE BEEN SHRINKING"
Identify places such as:

- Ministry
- Leadership

- Relationships
- Creativity
- Expression
- Decision-making
- Testimony
- Personal calling

____

____

____

____

SECTION 2: "HOW I WILL SHOW UP BOLDLY"

Write specific steps you will take to show up fully and authentically this week. Boldness is built through intentional action.

____

____

____

____

IDENTITY & VOICE ACTIVATION

Speak these declarations aloud; your spirit needs to hear your voice:

- "I will no longer shrink to make others comfortable."
- "I show up boldly because God is with me."
- "I am becoming the fullest expression of who God made me."
- "Fear has no place in my identity."
- "I live boldly, authentically, and unapologetically, on purpose."

Now write your own declaration beginning with: "I refuse to dim my light because…"

Let truth rise as you finish this sentence.

____

____

APPLICATION EXERCISE: REDEFINING THE REAL YOU

Use the space below to draw two circles side by side.

CIRCLE 1: "WHO I HAVE BEEN"

List traits shaped by fear, insecurity, or past experiences.

Examples:

- Quieting myself
- Playing small
- People-pleasing
- Hiding my gifts
- Staying in the background

CIRCLE 2: "WHO I AM BECOMING"

List traits shaped by identity, boldness, and authenticity.

Examples:
- Courageous
- Confident
- Clear-voiced
- Authentic
- Purpose-driven
- Unapologetically myself

Now draw an arrow from Circle 1 to Circle 2. Label it "My Becoming Journey."

LIVING OUT LOUD CHECK-IN

How boldly are you living this week?

Rate yourself:

AREA	1	2	3	4	5
I no longer shrink in fear or insecurity.	☐	☐	☐	☐	☐
I feel more confident living authentically.	☐	☐	☐	☐	☐
I show up boldly in the spaces God calls me to.	☐	☐	☐	☐	☐
I live in alignment with my identity and purpose.	☐	☐	☐	☐	☐

GROWTH THOUGHT FOR THE WEEK

Living out loud for God isn't about making noise. It's about making Him known.

CLOSING PRAYER

Lord, stretch my courage. Break every fear that caused me to shrink, hide, or dim my light. Redefine my confidence, reshape my boldness, and help me show up fully in every space You have called me to. Let my life shine, not for my glory, but for Yours. I choose to live out loud. I choose to live on purpose. Amen.

LIVING OUT LOUD PAGES

Write honestly. Speak freely. Respond intentionally.

Write about a moment when you lived out loud, even in a small way, and how it changed something in or around you.

CHAPTER 11

THE FRUIT THAT REMAINS: LEGACY OF LOUD LIVING

REFLECTION WARM-UP

Before you begin, pause and reflect:

- What kind of impact do you want your life to make?
- What "fruit" in your life is visible right now, and what fruit is missing?
- Are you living for temporary affirmation or eternal impact?

You were created for a legacy. The fruit of your life is meant to outlive you.

CHAPTER SUMMARY

God never designed your purpose to be temporary. You were created to bear lasting fruit, fruit that changes lives, influences generations, and reflects the character of Christ.

This chapter reminds you that true fruit is not measured by applause, accomplishments, or titles. Fruit is seen in your love, obedience, consistency, character, prayers, kindness, influence, service, and spiritual maturity.

Lasting fruit comes from abiding, staying connected to God, rooted in His Word, and aligned with His will. As you walk out your purpose, God produces fruit in you and through you that remains long after seasons change and people come and go. Your life is meant to leave a mark. Your obedience is meant to leave a legacy.

KEY TAKEAWAYS

- Lasting fruit comes from intimacy with God, not striving.
- Your legacy is formed by daily obedience, not big moments.
- God desires your life to produce fruit that influences others.
- Spiritual fruit is eternal; it outlives circumstances and seasons.

SCRIPTURE FOUNDATION

- "If you remain in Me… you will bear much fruit" (John 15:5).
- The fruit of the Spirit (Galatians 5:22-23).
- A fruitful tree planted by rivers of water (Psalm 1:3).
- Good trees produce good fruit (Matthew 7:17).

REFLECTION QUESTIONS

Reflect deeply; legacy requires intentionality.

What spiritual fruit (love, joy, peace, etc.) is most visible in your life right now?

____

____

____

____

Which fruit needs more cultivation or consistency?

____

____

____

____

What has your life produced in others so far?

____

____

____

____

What legacy do you want to leave for your family, ministry, or community?

____

____

____

____

What small daily choices help you bear more fruit?

____

____

____

____

PURPOSE PRACTICE

The Fruit Assessment

Rate each fruit of the Spirit from 1-5 based on how strongly it appears in your life right now.

- Love
- Joy
- Peace
- Patience
- Kindness

- Goodness
- Faithfulness
- Gentleness
- Self-Control

Circle the two that need the most growth.

Write one practical step you can take this week to strengthen each area.

____

____

____

____

Fruit grows through intentional habits.

IDENTITY & VOICE ACTIVATION

Declare these truths aloud:

- "My life will produce fruit that matters."
- "I am consistent, rooted, and stable in Christ."
- "My obedience is planting seeds for future genera-tions."
- "I bear fruit that remains."

Complete this sentence:
"The fruit I want my life to be known for is_____________,"

(Examples: compassion, faithfulness, integrity, wisdom, courage, love, generosity.)

Let God lead your heart as you write.

____

____

APPLICATION EXERCISE: MY LEGACY LIST

Draw two sections:

SECTION 1: "WHAT I WANT MY LIFE TO PRODUCE"

List the spiritual, emotional, and relational fruit you desire to cultivate.

Examples:

- A family rooted in faith
- A life of generosity
- A ministry that transforms others
- A reputation of kindness
- A legacy of prayer

____

____

____

____

SECTION 2: "SEEDS I CAN PLANT TODAY"

For each item above, write a small action that plants that fruit now.

Example:

- Fruit: A legacy of faith
- Seed: Pray consistently for your children

____

____

____

____

Legacy is built one seed at a time.

LIVING OUT LOUD CHECK-IN

How intentional are you about your spiritual legacy?

Rate yourself:

AREA	1	2	3	4	5
I am cultivating the fruit of the Spirit in my life.	☐	☐	☐	☐	☐
I am aware of the legacy I want to leave.	☐	☐	☐	☐	☐
My daily habits reflect my long-term purpose.	☐	☐	☐	☐	☐
I believe God is producing lasting fruit in me.	☐	☐	☐	☐	☐

GROWTH THOUGHT FOR THE WEEK

Your legacy is not what you accumulate. It is what you activate in others

CLOSING PRAYER

Lord, produce lasting fruit in my life. Help me remain connected to You so that my actions, character, and obedience reflect Your heart. Teach me to sow intentionally, love deeply, give freely, and live purposefully. Let my life leave a legacy that honors You, one that impacts generations and brings glory to Your name. Amen.

LIVING OUT LOUD PAGES

Write honestly. Speak freely. Respond intentionally.

Write about someone whose life has produced fruit that impacted you, and what you hope to emulate.

CHAPTER 12

DAVID WAS A MORNING PERSON

REFLECTION WARM-UP

Before you begin, settle your heart.

Ask yourself:

- How do I usually start my mornings, rushed, distracted, or centered?
- What would my life look like if I consistently began my day with God?
- What gets in the way of prioritizing spiritual rhythm?

This chapter invites you to slow down, rise intentionally, and meet God early.

CHAPTER SUMMARY

David had a pattern; he sought God *early*. He did so before responsibilities, demands, people, or his emotions took over. He positioned his heart before God at the start of each day, creating rhythm, stability, and intimacy with the Father.

This chapter shows that becoming a "morning person" is not about personality; it's about priority. When you begin your day in God's presence, everything else aligns. Your perspective shifts. Your emotions stabilize. Your decisions become sharper. Your spirit becomes rooted.

God doesn't just want your leftover time; He desires your first time. The morning is where clarity, peace, and purpose begin.

KEY TAKEAWAYS

- Morning devotion grounds your day in God's presence.
- Seeking God early creates confidence, stability, and spiritual clarity.
- A morning rhythm is a spiritual discipline, not a personality trait.
- Your life aligns more fully when God is the first voice you hear.

SCRIPTURE FOUNDATION

- In the morning, I direct my prayer to You (Psalm 5:3).
- Early will I seek You (Psalm 63:1).
- New mercies every morning (Lamentations 3:22-23).
- Jesus rose early to pray (Mark 1:3).

REFLECTION QUESTIONS

Reflect honestly; morning habits often reveal spiritual priorities.

What emotions or distractions typically control your mornings?

How do your mornings affect the rest of your day?

What keeps you from starting your day with God?

What would change if you made morning devotion a consistent habit?

____

____

____

____

Where do you sense God inviting you to slow down, rise early, or prioritize Him?

____

____

____

____

PURPOSE PRACTICE

Build Your Morning Rhythm

Fill in each section to create a simple, consistent spiritual routine:

1. TIME

What time will you wake or set aside for devotion?

____

____

____

____

2. SPACE

Where will you meet with God each morning?

____

____

____

____

3. SCRIPTURE

Choose one verse or chapter to meditate on this week.

____

____

____

____

4. PRAYER FOCUS

What will you pray about or seek God for?

____

____

____

____

5. PRACTICE

What spiritual discipline will you engage in?

____

____

____

____

(Examples: worship, journaling, silence, gratitude, intercession.)

Creating structure builds consistency.

IDENTITY & VOICE ACTIVATION

Speak these declarations:

- "I rise to meet God before I meet the world."
- "My mornings belong to God."

- "Seeking God early sets the tone for my day."
- "My discipline is growing; my spirit is strengthening."

Now write:
"My intention for morning devotion is…"

____

____

Let this intention guide your new rhythm.

APPLICATION EXERCISE: MORNING BARRIERS & BREAKTHROUGHS
Complete the two sections:

SECTION 1: "MY BARRIERS"
List anything that makes it hard to start your day with God.

Examples:
- Fatigue
- Phone distractions
- Busy schedule
- Lack of focus
- Inconsistency
- Emotional heaviness

____

____

____

____

SECTION 2: "MY BREAKTHROUGH STRATEGIES"

Write practical steps to overcome each barrier.

Examples:

- Set out Bible and journal the night before.
- Charge phone in a different room.
- Pray before getting out of bed.
- Go to bed earlier.
- Use a morning worship playlist.

____

____

____

____

This turns frustration into strategy.

LIVING OUT LOUD CHECK-IN

How aligned are your mornings with God right now?

Rate yourself:

AREA	1 2 3 4 5
I desire to seek God early.	☐ ☐ ☐ ☐ ☐

AREA   **1 2 3 4 5**

I am creating a consistent morning rhythm.   ☐ ☐ ☐ ☐ ☐

I hear God's voice more clearly when I start
with Him.   ☐ ☐ ☐ ☐ ☐

My mornings set the tone for my day in a pos-
itive way.   ☐ ☐ ☐ ☐ ☐

GROWTH THOUGHT FOR THE WEEK

Living out loud begins in the secret place long before it shows up in public.

CLOSING PRAYER

Lord, teach me to seek You early. Reset my rhythm. Strengthen my discipline. Awaken my spirit with Your presence each morning. Let my day begin with Your voice, Your Word, peace, and direction. Help me cultivate a morning pattern that aligns me with Your purpose. Amen.

LIVING OUT LOUD PAGES

Write honestly. Speak freely. Respond intentionally.

Write about a time when God spoke to you or strengthened you early in the morning, or write what you hope morning devotion will bring into your life.

CHAPTER 13

THE MOST POWERFUL CHURCH IS AN INTENTIONAL CHURCH

REFLECTION WARM-UP

Before you begin, pause and reflect:

- What does *church* truly mean to you?
- Do you see yourself as a participant or a spectator?
- How intentional are you about your role in the body of Christ?

The church is not a building you attend; it is a body you belong to.

CHAPTER SUMMARY

When individuals who are committed to living out loud on purpose come together in unity, something powerful happens. They become the church as God designed it to be—not passive, reactive, or routine-driven but intentional.

Jesus declared in Matthew 16:18 that He would build His church and that the gates of hell would not prevail against it. That promise is attached to a church that knows who it is, understands its mission, and moves with purpose.

An intentional church does not wait for revival; it cultivates it. It does not chase trends; it establishes kingdom culture. It does not simply fill seats; it fills lives with transformation.

The strength of the church is found in the intentionality of its people. When believers live out loud in their personal callings and unite in purpose, the church becomes a powerful, Spirit-led force that transforms communities and advances the kingdom of God.

Your purpose is not only personal; it is corporate. Your obedience strengthens the whole body.

KEY TAKEAWAYS

- The most powerful church is not the loudest, largest, or flashiest; it is the most intentional.
- The church is built by committed people, not passive attendees.
- Every believer has a role that strengthens the body.
- Intentional discipleship produces lasting spiritual impact.
- Unity multiplies power.

SCRIPTURE FOUNDATION

- "I will build My church, and the gates of hell shall not prevail against it" (Matthew 16:18).

- The early church lived with devotion, unity, and purpose (Acts 2:42-47).
- Every part does its work so the body grows in love (Ephesians 4:16).
- You are the body of Christ, and each one is a part (1 Corinthians 12:27).

REFLECTION QUESTIONS

Answer honestly and prayerfully:

How are you currently contributing to the intentionality of your church?

____

____

____

____

In what ways can you live more purposefully within your faith community?

____

____

____

____

What role or "part of the body" has God uniquely called you to strengthen?

____

____

____

____

How can you help your church move beyond routine into transformation?

____

____

____

____

Are you showing up with intention—or simply out of habit?

____

____

____

____

PURPOSE PRACTICE

From Attender to Builder

Complete the following:

I currently contribute to my church by:

____

____

____

____

One area where God is calling me to be more intentional is:

____

____

____

____

One step I can take this month to strengthen the body is:

____

____

____

____

Intentional churches are built by intentional people.

IDENTITY & VOICE ACTIVATION

Speak these declarations aloud:

- "I am not just attending church; I am part of the body."
- "My purpose strengthens the whole church."
- "I show up with intention, not routine."
- "God uses my obedience to advance His kingdom."

Now write your own declaration:

"I commit to being an intentional part of the body of Christ by…"

____

____

____

APPLICATION EXERCISE: THE INTENTIONAL CHURCH MAP

Answer the questions in the three sections that follow.

1. MY GIFTS & STRENGTHS

What abilities, experiences, or spiritual gifts has God given you?

____

____

____

2. WHERE THE CHURCH NEEDS STRENGTH

Where do you see opportunities for growth, service, or discipleship?

____

____

____

3. WHERE I CAN SERVE WITH PURPOSE

How can your gifts meet the needs of the body?

____

____

____

____

This is how intentional churches are built — alignment of gifts and mission.

LIVING OUT LOUD CHECK-IN

Rate yourself:

AREA	1	2	3	4	5
I see myself as part of the body, not just an attendee.	☐	☐	☐	☐	☐
I serve with intention rather than obligation.	☐	☐	☐	☐	☐
I understand how my purpose impacts the church.	☐	☐	☐	☐	☐
I am committed to spiritual growth and discipleship.	☐	☐	☐	☐	☐

GROWTH THOUGHT FOR THE WEEK

Your purpose isn't only personal; it's corporate.

CLOSING PRAYER

Heavenly Father, thank You for calling me into Your body, the church. Help me live and serve with intention, not routine. Strengthen me to play my part, love deeply, and advance Your kingdom. Make us a church that is not only powerful in word but intentional in deed. Let our lives reflect Your glory together. In Jesus' name. Amen.

LIVING OUT LOUD PAGES
Write honestly. Speak freely. Respond intentionally.

What would change in my church if every believer lived out loud on purpose, including me?

____

____

____

____

____

____

____

____

____

____

____

BONUS ACTIVATION
CHAPTER 14

WALK IT OUT

REFLECTION WARM-UP

Take a deep breath. This is your moment. Ask yourself:

- What has God awakened in me through this journey?
- What do I know now about myself that I didn't know before?
- What is the next step God is calling me to take?

Let this be a sacred pause—a moment of clarity and commitment.

CHAPTER PURPOSE

This final chapter brings everything together: your identity, voice, purpose, becoming, boldness, discipline, legacy, resilience, and call.

Now that God has revealed who you are and what He has placed within you, it's time to *walk it out.*

CHAPTER SUMMARY

Purpose is not fulfilled through inspiration alone; it requires movement. This chapter is about stepping forward, making decisions, applying all you've learned, and living your purpose consistently and courageously.

You are no longer the version of yourself who began this workbook. You have shed old labels. You have reclaimed your voice. You have confronted fear, fire, and identity.
You have built rhythm, embraced sacrifice, and defined your legacy. Now God is asking you to move, act, and walk boldly into the future He designed for you.

Walking it out means:

- Taking small daily steps
- Obeying God consistently
- Trusting God even when the road is unfamiliar
- Using what He placed inside you
- Showing up boldly
- Living authentically
- Remaining connected to the Source
- Staying committed to the journey

This chapter is your commissioning moment. Your purpose is not theoretical; it is *walked out*.

KEY TAKEAWAYS

- Purpose demands action, not just understanding.
- You must walk out what God revealed to you in this season.

- Daily obedience leads to supernatural breakthrough.
- You already possess what you need for this next step.
- God walks with you as you walk out His assignment.

SCRIPTURE FOUNDATION

- Be doers of the Word, not hearers only (James 1:22).
- The steps of a good person are ordered by the Lord (Psalm 37:23).
- Be strong, courageous, and obedient (Joshua 1:7-9).
- Write the vision; make it plain (Habakkuk 2:2).

REFLECTION QUESTIONS

Reflect boldly; this is your activation moment.

What step is God asking you to take that you have been avoiding?

____

____

____

____

What have you learned about yourself on this journey?

____

____

What fears remain, and what truths overpower them?

What relationships, habits, or mindsets must you adjust to walk in purpose?

What is one practical action you can take this week to move in purpose?

____

____

PURPOSE PRACTICE

Write Your Purpose Plan

Over the next 30 days, what steps will you commit to taking? Write 1-3 steps in each category and assign a date.

Purpose grows through consistent movement.

1. SPIRITUAL STEPS

(prayer, Bible study, community, fasting, devotion)

____

____

____

____

2. PERSONAL STEPS

(health, boundaries, habits, self-care, emotional growth)

____

3. PURPOSE STEPS

(launching something, finishing something, showing up boldly)

____

____

____

____

____

____

____

____

____

IDENTITY & VOICE ACTIVATION

Speak these declarations with authority:

- "I am ready."
- "I have what I need."
- "I walk in purpose without fear."
- "What God started in me, I will continue."
- "I walk boldly, faithfully, and intentionally."
- "The next step is mine to take."

Now write your own commissioning statement: "Today, I commit to walking out my purpose by…"

____

____

Let this be your covenant with yourself and God.

APPLICATION EXERCISE: THE ACTIVATION MAP
"My Next Step Map"

Use the space below to write your response. If you need more room, feel free to continue on a separate sheet of paper or in a journal.

What God revealed to me

____

____

____

____

What I must release

____

____

____

____

What I must pursue

____

____

____

____

My next immediate step

____

____

____

____

This map becomes your guide for the next chapter of your life.

LIVING OUT LOUD CHECK-IN

Are you ready to walk out your purpose?

Rate yourself:

AREA	1	2	3	4	5
I am committed to taking my next step.	☐	☐	☐	☐	☐
I feel equipped to walk in my purpose.	☐	☐	☐	☐	☐
I believe God is guiding my steps.	☐	☐	☐	☐	☐
I am prepared to live out loud in this next season.	☐	☐	☐	☐	☐

GROWTH THOUGHT FOR THE WEEK

Living out loud on purpose means choosing to live as someone who has discovered that God has a purpose for you, and you are His purpose.

CLOSING PRAYER

Father, thank You for every revelation, healing, and breakthrough in this journey. Thank You for restoring my identity, strengthening my voice, and revealing my purpose. As I walk into my next steps, order my path. Guide my decisions. Strengthen my obedience. Fill me with courage, clarity, and boldness. Help me live out loud, with intention, purpose, and unwavering faith. I am ready. I am willing. I am walking it out. Amen.

LIVING OUT LOUD PAGES

Write honestly. Speak freely. Respond intentionally.

MY PERSONAL COMMISSIONING

Write your heart out.
What is God calling you into?
What do you feel rising in you?
Where are you going from here?

____

____

____

____

____

____

____

____

____

____

CONCLUSION

You have reached the end of this workbook, but this is not the end of your journey. In fact, it is the beginning of a new chapter in your life, identity, voice, and calling.

Over these thirteen chapters (plus your brand-new bonus activation chapter), you have confronted fear, embraced identity, strengthened your voice, endured refining seasons, acknowledged the cost of your calling, cultivated spiritual discipline, and awakened to the purpose God placed within you.

This workbook was never about simply completing pages. It was about transformation. It was about peeling back layers of limitation, shame, silence, and doubt. It was about rediscovering the strength and brilliance God placed in you. It was about healing, stretching, growing, and stepping forward with courage.

As you close this workbook:

- You are walking differently.
- You are thinking differently.

- You are believing differently.
- You are speaking differently.
- You are living differently.

The quiet, hidden version of you is no longer in charge. Purpose is calling. Identity is rising. Your voice is no longer optional; it is necessary. Carry what you learned into your home, ministry, workplace, and community. Walk boldly. Walk intentionally. Walk authentically. Walk faithfully. Walk purposefully.

And remember:
You are not walking alone.
Every step is ordered.
Every move is guided.
Every assignment is empowered by the Holy Spirit.
This is your moment.
This is your season.
This is your call.

Now… go live out loud. On purpose. For purpose. With purpose. Amen.

FACILITATOR NOTES APPENDIX

For Group Leaders, Ministers, Mentors & Small Group Facilitators

HOW TO USE THE FACILITATOR NOTES

This appendix gives additional guidance for leading small groups, classes, workshops, or ministry cohorts through *Living Out Loud on Purpose!*

These notes are NOT meant to replace the participant experience but to enhance group connection and deepen spiritual formation.

Each section includes:

- Teaching Overview – a quick summary to introduce the lesson
- Key Insights to Emphasize
- Discussion Questions (beyond workbook prompts)
- Facilitator Cautions, boundaries, emotional care, sensitivity
- Group Activities or Exercises
- Prayer Focus

Use what fits your group. Adapt where necessary. Allow the Holy Spirit to guide.

CHAPTER 1: YOU DID THAT ON PURPOSE

TEACHING OVERVIEW

Introduce the importance of spiritual and emotional awareness. This chapter helps participants recognize areas where they may have been dormant, distracted, or stagnant.

KEY INSIGHTS

- Awareness is the doorway to transformation.
- What is not acknowledged cannot be changed.
- God awakens us with intention and care.

DISCUSSION ADDITIONS

- When did you realize you were "asleep" in an area of your life?
- What helped spark your spiritual awakening?

FACILITATOR CAUTIONS

This chapter may surface regret or grief; lead with grace and reassurance.

GROUP ACTIVITY

Invite participants to name one area where they sense God awakening.

PRAYER FOCUS

Awakening, clarity, and spiritual sensitivity.

CHAPTER 2: PURPOSE: THE AGE-OLD QUESTION

TEACHING OVERVIEW

Guide participants in identifying internal barriers, fears, and unspoken struggles connected to purpose.

KEY INSIGHTS

- Naming struggles weakens shame's power.
- Honesty opens the door to healing.

DISCUSSION ADDITIONS

- Why is it difficult to name personal struggles?
- How can this group foster safety and trust?

FACILITATOR CAUTIONS

Do not pressure vulnerability; honor each person's readiness.

GROUP ACTIVITY

Participants write one word representing a struggle on a sticky note and discard it as a symbolic release.

PRAYER FOCUS

Courage, honesty, and truth.

CHAPTER 3: BECOMING: EMBRACING THE PROCESS OF PURPOSE

TEACHING OVERVIEW

Reinforce that becoming is a process shaped over time, not a destination reached overnight.

KEY INSIGHTS

- Growth unfolds in seasons.
- Hidden seasons are often the most formative.

DISCUSSION ADDITIONS

- Which area of your becoming requires the most patience?

FACILITATOR CAUTIONS

Some may feel delayed or behind; remind them God redeems every season.

GROUP ACTIVITY

Have participants write a brief Becoming Statement and share one sentence.

PRAYER FOCUS

Patience, grace, and transformation.

CHAPTER 4: ON DISPLAY: WHEN PURPOSE GOES PUBLIC

TEACHING OVERVIEW

Explore how God places His people in visible spaces for impact, not ego.

KEY INSIGHTS

- Visibility is an assignment, not self-promotion.
- Being seen can serve and strengthen others.

DISCUSSION ADDITIONS

- What fears surface when God brings you into visibility?
- How can the group offer support during visible seasons?

FACILITATOR CAUTIONS

Be mindful of those who feel overlooked or unseen.

GROUP ACTIVITY

Role-play healthy responses to moments of visibility.

PRAYER FOCUS

Courage, humility, and faithfulness.

CHAPTER 5: RESPONDING VS. REACTING: LIVING WITH DISCERNMENT AND DISCIPLINE

TEACHING OVERVIEW

Teach that emotional maturity is a vital expression of spiritual maturity.

KEY INSIGHTS

- Reactions are emotion-driven; responses are wisdom-led.
- The Holy Spirit empowers self-control.

DISCUSSION ADDITIONS

- What helps you pause before reacting?

FACILITATOR CAUTIONS

Handle trauma-related triggers with sensitivity and care.

GROUP ACTIVITY

Practice the PAUSE tool together as a response strategy.

PRAYER FOCUS

Self-control, healing, and wisdom.

CHAPTER 6: IDENTITY: REMEMBER WHO YOU ARE

TEACHING OVERVIEW

Affirm that identity is spiritual and foundational to purpose.

KEY INSIGHTS

- God defines identity, not pain or people.
- Identity conflicts are spiritual battles.

DISCUSSION ADDITIONS

- What false label has been hardest to release?

FACILITATOR CAUTIONS

Identity wounds can be deep; invite the Holy Spirit's presence.

GROUP ACTIVITY

Participants write two identity truths on index cards.

PRAYER FOCUS

Identity restoration and confidence.

CHAPTER 7: VOICE: YOU WERE NEVER MEANT TO BE SILENT

TEACHING OVERVIEW

Encourage participants to reclaim voices that have been silenced by fear, trauma, or doubt.

KEY INSIGHTS

- Your voice carries spiritual authority.
- Testimony brings freedom.

DISCUSSION ADDITIONS

- Who needs to hear your voice right now?

FACILITATOR CAUTIONS

Be sensitive to past experiences involving silencing.

GROUP ACTIVITY

Voice activation circle: each participant shares a 10-second declaration.

PRAYER FOCUS

Boldness, clarity, and healing of the voice.

CHAPTER 8: FIREPROOF: STANDING WHEN IT'S HARD

TEACHING OVERVIEW

Reframe trials as refining experiences rather than destructive ones.

KEY INSIGHTS

- Fire reveals strength and character.

- God is present in every trial.

DISCUSSION ADDITIONS

- What strength did a past trial produce in you?

FACILITATOR CAUTIONS

Honor vulnerability and protect confidentiality.

GROUP ACTIVITY

Create a collective visual "refining map."

PRAYER FOCUS

Strength, endurance, and comfort.

CHAPTER 9: LIVING OUT LOUD: THE COST OF THE CALL

TEACHING OVERVIEW

Acknowledge that purpose requires sacrifice and obedience.

KEY INSIGHTS

- Sacrifice prepares us for purpose.
- Obedience unlocks destiny.

DISCUSSION ADDITIONS

- What has following God cost you?

FACILITATOR CAUTIONS

Affirm sacrifices without comparison or pressure.

GROUP ACTIVITY

Voluntary sharing from a Surrender Inventory.

PRAYER FOCUS

Trust, obedience, and surrender.

CHAPTER 10: LIVING OUT LOUD: REDEFINED

TEACHING OVERVIEW

Clarify that boldness flows from authenticity, not performance.

KEY INSIGHTS

- Living out loud is alignment, not attention-seeking.
- Authenticity liberates others.

DISCUSSION ADDITIONS

- How can you live more authentically this week?

FACILITATOR CAUTIONS

Avoid equating boldness with extroversion.

GROUP ACTIVITY

Create two lists: "Where I Shrink" and "How I Rise."

PRAYER FOCUS

Courage, authenticity, and boldness.

CHAPTER 11: THE FRUIT THAT REMAINS: LEGACY OF LOUD LIVING

TEACHING OVERVIEW

Teach that legacy is shaped through daily faithfulness.

KEY INSIGHTS

- Fruit reflects character, not accomplishments.
- Legacy extends beyond a lifetime.

DISCUSSION ADDITIONS

- What fruit do you want to leave for the next generation?

FACILITATOR CAUTIONS

Address grief with hope and forward vision.

GROUP ACTIVITY

Create a group legacy map.

PRAYER FOCUS

Fruitfulness, consistency, and generational impact.

CHAPTER 12: DAVID WAS A MORNING PERSON

TEACHING OVERVIEW

Highlight how intentional rhythms strengthen spiritual life.

KEY INSIGHTS

- Morning devotion anchors the day.
- Discipline reinforces identity.

DISCUSSION ADDITIONS

- What could one consistent morning habit change?

FACILITATOR CAUTIONS

Avoid guilt-based motivation; emphasize grace.

GROUP ACTIVITY

Design a personal morning rhythm together.

PRAYER FOCUS

Discipline, intimacy, and spiritual rhythm.

CHAPTER 13: THE MOST POWERFUL CHURCH IS AN INTENTIONAL CHURCH

TEACHING OVERVIEW

Emphasize that the church is not a building, but a body made strong through intentional people living out loud together.

KEY INSIGHTS

- The strength of the church is rooted in intentionality, not size or style.
- Every believer has a role that strengthens the whole body.
- Personal obedience produces corporate power.

DISCUSSION ADDITIONS

- Do you see yourself more as a participant or a spectator in the church?
- Where is God calling you to be more intentional in the body?

FACILITATOR CAUTIONS

Avoid guilt-driven language; focus on invitation, purpose, and empowerment.

GROUP ACTIVITY

Have participants identify one way they can move from routine to intentional engagement this month.

PRAYER FOCUS

Unity, obedience, and intentional discipleship.

BONUS ACTIVATION CHAPTER 14: WALK IT OUT

TEACHING OVERVIEW

This chapter activates participants to move forward in purpose.

KEY INSIGHTS

- Purpose requires action.
- God directs intentional steps.

DISCUSSION ADDITIONS

- What is your next realistic step of obedience?

FACILITATOR CAUTIONS

Encourage progress without overwhelming expectations.

GROUP ACTIVITY

Create and share an Activation Map.

PRAYER FOCUS

Activation, clarity, and commissioning.

THE VISUAL METAPHOR
OF LIVING OUT LOUD ON PURPOSE

The cover of *Living Out Loud on Purpose* is a visual metaphor of the spiritual transformation that occurs when you stop shrinking, start shining, and boldly walk in alignment with God's divine plan.

The front cover, with its vivid paint splashes, represents a life filled with motion, emotion, and potential—but lacking clarity. It captures what it feels like to exist without truly living: colorful, expressive, yet undefined. It mirrors the season many go through—playing supportive roles, staying silent in rooms where they were meant to speak, hiding behind expectations instead of walking in purpose. This is what life looks like before we find our voice, embrace our God-given identity, and begin walking in alignment with heaven.

The back cover tells a different story—the one God always intended. The same colors now take on new form and meaning, transforming into a **flower, butterfly, tree, and bird,** each a symbol of a believer awakened to their divine calling:

- The **flower** represents spiritual blooming—what happens when you stop hiding and begin to flourish in the soil of God's Word (Psalm 1:3).
- The **butterfly** reflects the beauty of transformation through Christ, as we are renewed in mind and spirit (Romans 12:2).
- The **tree** symbolizes strength, stability, and a life rooted in purpose, bearing fruit that impacts generations (Jeremiah 17:7–8).
- The **bird** embodies freedom in Christ and the boldness to rise above fear and walk by faith (Isaiah 40:31).

Together, these images reflect what happens when you choose to live out loud on purpose—with clarity, courage, and conviction. You stop echoing the world and start embodying the kingdom.

This cover is more than a design—it's a declaration. It says:

"I will not shrink to fit spaces God called me to transform. I will rise. I will speak. I will live on purpose."

And just like the message inside the book, it invites every reader to move from invisibility to intentionality, from hiding to holy boldness, from silence to significance—through the power of knowing who you are, whose you are, and why you're here.

ABOUT THE AUTHOR

Karen F. Hatcher, M.S. in Marriage and Family Therapy, is a National Evangelist in the Church Of God In Christ. A devoted wife, mother, and grandmother, she blends her passion for faith, family, and service with wisdom and authenticity.

Evangelist Hatcher has dedicated her life to strengthening individuals and families by integrating mental health, spirituality, and biblical principles. Her mission is to empower the body of Christ to fulfill God's purpose in this generation, boldly proclaiming that the kingdom of heaven is at hand and urging believers to prepare for the soon-coming King. She serves as the First Lady of Miracle Temple of Deliverance Church Of God In Christ in Louisville, Kentucky, alongside her husband, Bishop Gabriel J. Hatcher Sr. Together, they are blessed with three children, Gabriel II, Sarah, and Rachel, and eleven grandchildren.